NOAH'S BOAT

NOAH'S **BOAT**

A Compendium of Beasties Large and Small

Poems by

CB FOLLETT

Many Voices Press
Flathead Valley Community College

with special thanks to

Tania Baban, Joyce Koskenmaki, Jim Natal,
David St. John, Susan Terris, Cloud View
Poets, Freeedom Writers, friends and supporters.
Our connectedness means so much to me.

Cover & Book Design by Tania Baban Natal
    www.confluxpress.com
Front cover painting, *Bear in a Boat,* and inside drawings
    © Joyce Koskenmaki / www.JoyceKoskenmaki.com

Back cover art by CB Follett www.arctospress.com

ISBN: 978-0-9833679-1-8

Library of Congress Control Number 2016940526
1. Poetry 2. Poetry-Follett, CB 3. Animals-Poetry
4. Nature-Poetry 5. Environment-Poetry
6. Poetry-United States-21st Century

Printed in the United States of America

Many Voices Press
Flathead Valley Community Press
777 Grandview Drive
Kalispell, Montana 59901
www.fvcc.edu

FOR LEE, MY FAVORITE CRITTER, ALWAYS

TABLE OF CONTENTS

CONNECTION

Linked with silken chains,
from the great blue whale struggling
to provide another link in his line
of existence
to tiny crawling things that I
may never know exist,
linked to me in ways
I cannot want to change.
Each loss,
those I feel and scream for,
those I'll never know,
impact me as I
unknowing impact them.
We will always be linked
or the whole complexity
will fall to ashes
on the blow of *what*:
politics carelessness
selfishness foolishness
all those 'nesses that threaten
what was once a world in balance?

Uh, Noah, Looks As If We Need You Again

And the old man, extremely old, a thin strip
of man shuffles outside and looks
up at the sky, getting a face full of downpour,
days of it.

And Noah smiles, turns to his left
and lifts his hammer from the prongs,
to his right for the sack of pegs and calls his sons
to come and haul back the planks from the hill.

As the rivers increase into torrents and where
there are no rivers, creeks are building, and where
there are no creeks the clay is alive with the tributaries
of brooklets, and Noah straightens his shoulders,
lifts his face to thank God for this good day
and sets to work.

He lays out the cubits, pulling a branch behind him
as he counts. He figures the cross-staves needed,
and calls Ham to bring down the curved ribs of gopher wood
he saved last time, when there were unicorns.

And he sends out Shem with the ram's horn
to alert the animals because water is increasing underfoot
and the skeletal boat already tugs to float free and the raven
arrives, and the dove, to squat on the blunt bowsprit
and supplies are needed, and bedding, and Mrs. Noah
screams from the house *Get inside you crazy old man.*
Let someone else do it this time.

And Noah grins, years falling
like layers of onion peeling down
to shiny new flesh, firm, full of zest

and along the ridges, animals begin to gather,
keeping high ground to let the sludge of cities
float by: telephones, their plastic receivers
bobbing like periscopes,
microwaves, toasters, blenders,
cords whipping behind them like snakes in the current

and Noah a blur of pounding, and rivers
rushing past to the sea: the Salinas, the Petaluma,
the Russian, all the bridges toppled now,
floating their boards and railings down to Noah's catch-all,
for floors, for mangers, grain cribs and for the gangplank,
as the days count toward forty.

ANIMAL DREAMS

They say
all mammals dream
and birds.
Into unconscious night
where colors and life-tales
are stored; where the heartbreaks
and triumphs of the waking world
are sorted to their good.

They cannot write their dreams.
Perhaps they celebrate in bird song,
one to the other,
until they have the kernel,
until they pad a little of the richness
of their dreams
onto their waking moments.

But not the reptiles:
turtles and snakes, alligators,
with their barren limbic brains
full of instinct and empty of poems.

All the time spent sunning on a log
at the edge of primordial ooze:
are there no daydreams
of the lacy wings of dragonflies?

ANTHROPOMORPHIA

Animals have no feelings, said the editor
returning my poem about hawks
that cruise the thermals,
they don't play.

Their sex lives are opportunistic.
Fickle, disloyal. The goose
who circles her shot mate
mournful as a dove.
Wolf, sea eagle, year after year
of monogamy.

Shouldn't we tell the children
that monkeys make snowballs and take sides,
that crows do loop de loops in the air
and barrel rolls, and that I have watched
a flock of them imitate the Blue Angels?

Otters lumber up a snowy slope
and toboggan down on their stomachs,
over and over. Crows too,
and stoat turned into ermine.

That dogs play for hours and will defend us
against danger; that three years after you left
our black lab raced the length of the beach
convinced it was you. And when she died,

the other dog mourned for a year, as elephants
mourn and if they can, bury the fallen,
as a gorilla in Palo Alto wailed
over the death of All Ball, her pet kitten.

ST. FRANCIS DAY

At Grace Cathedral

In honor of St. Francis, his arms
extended to all the living,
legged and rooted,
pews teem with cold noses, loyal eyes.
Dogs, cats, human and bird notes
rise like doves to the high X of the nave,
a beekeeper raises his frame to the blessing
and a San Francisco policeman leads his horse
before the high altar.

Light winks off well-groomed heads,
rhinestone collars, bows jaunty
around hairy necks. We pat them
and they give us the gladness
of their willingness to please.

But no salmon are there, dolphins
or manatees. Who blesses the spotted owl,
elephant, the blue mountain butterfly,
who calls *brother* the belt of frogs
gone missing around the globe?

Those others
who need some share of earth
but do not look at us adoringly
do not beg to be petted;
each tree felled — a microcosm
of the great and small interwoven
and we a part of the silk
that keeps the web afloat — you
cannot make a web with just one spoke.

Where can we take our children to see
how the world works without man's
sharpened scythe,
where air and water interchange
and ancient draped trees still exist.

ANEMONES AT POINT LOBOS

The wave shatters its tidal sweep
against outcrops of rock,
shovels into crevices, glissades
off the smoothed green slopes
of serpentine; it breathes
into tide pools
driving blue crabs to cower
clicking fore-claws
in their hurry for a tight crack.

Anemones like Easter bonnets
lean with the surge,
blazing their pink feathers
at whatever the wave brings them.
As it retreats, wands bend
with its going, stroking through froth
for some last morsel.

And in a moment of clear stillness
the next wave gathers.

ARMADILLO ON A TEXAS ROAD

okay
I can make it
across the road
early morning
traffic light, but
I'm not very fast.
and for some I'm just
another moving target.
here goes
caught the wind draft of that one
right where uncle irwin got it
don't linger
don't think about it
so many cousins, three
aunts and two uncles
splotched
just this year.
ooh that was close
a little farther dang
tire graze
curled me into a ball
rolled back a bit
scurry now
plates creaking
paws getting hot
whoosh another
thanks for avoiding me
nice driver nice driver
there made it across
the north bound lanes

a bit of grass
catch my breath
why do I even try you ask
simple she lives

on the other side
it's that season
have to try
okay, south bound
whoosh whoosh
uh oh some undertow on that last one

I'm almost there
I think I see her by that lone tree
here goes
just one more lane to love

ANTELOPE

Wouldn't it spin the planets, if antelope had done
the cave paintings? A necromancy of all their relatives
brought down by spears and arrows.

Look, there's great-grandmother leading the charge,
just before they trample that puny cave person.
And it's not fair. We outrun just as many as Old
Saber Tooth, but he gets to eat them, smacking his
lips over the tender bits. We're stuck with this
spiky yellow stuff, bristly and full of chaff. Yuck.
Only time it's decent is when it's wet and green.
Then at least you can chew the damn stuff. Hey!
Watch it with that torchiere. You just singed my
inner left point and made me jog on this portrait
of great Aunt Bossie and give her a rump like an
elephant. Now she'll be haunting this cave for eons
with her foul ruminant breath. Come on. The Muse
has left me. Let's stampede.

WHILE SHEPHERDS TEND THEIR FLOCKS

Sister ants corral their aphids and tenderly
stroke their backs. The aphids, sybaritic
to the core, obligingly evacuate their lovely fecal
grains of sugary water, so relished
by the colony. The sisters tend their flock
clustered on the broad blades of mule ears.
Their sheep suck from the leaves. The
shepherds reap the crop and carry it off
to their home in the hill. All are pleased.

Mule ear chewed to lace, it's time to move on.
The sisterhood converges, each lifts an aphid
from its exhausted lunch table and caries it
over the sward of green to the next pasture
a sort of progressive dinner. The ants
provide the salad. The aphids eat
and provide the sorbet.

If I

were a bird,
it would be an Australian bowerbird.
Not the female, high on chivalry's plinth,
awaiting the espousal chamber.
No, *he* gets all the fun,
this feathered Bramante,
constructing his wedding court.
A bower of twigs, lined with grasses,
arching gothic high as seven feet.
Trussed and interwoven
against the wooing dance.

His, too, the decorative arts.
Bright bits of string, shells, and berries,
iridescent insect wings,
whatever the wind brings his field palette.
Scraps of tinfoil tucked here,
pebbles or a shilling there.
Using a twig dipped in berry,
he paints his Sistine Chapel,
gossamers it with spider's web,

steps back, considers, then
into niches and cracks,
he pushes fresh flowers,
replaced as needed.

The Gardener Bowerbird
sweeps clean his front porch,
and there, like a street peddler,
displays more bright and glittery treasures
arranged with a constant decorator's flutter.

She approaches.

He dances.
Charleston, jitterbug, aerobic.
Obsequious in his need for approval.
She, insufferable tease,
slowly inspects the bloomed bower,
pausing to stare into the distance
as if distracted.
Bewitched,
he settles a twig,
adds a feather.
And tries the tango.

Inspection now complete,
she eyes him carefully,
considering.
Oh, the anguish of his soul.

But she, too, is caressed by Spring,
an urgency that cannot be aloof.
Daintily, she steps inside.
It is done.

THE BUFFALO AND THE RED ROCK

There was a time when the land ran black with buffalo, when their hooves cut the ground into pocks of dry holes, when the dust of their passing occluded the sky, and the sun was lost through long afternoons, turning the air to a rust red, and the noise was like rivers headlong to the sea, shaking the continents, and buffalo were held sacred, driven deep in the myths of the plains, supplying robes and tents, meat and weapons, wool and stories. Their heads became headdresses; the people wore their horns, the poll, the shaggy masks in ceremonies, calling the gods out of the hills, and the red rock gave up its color for the walls of caves, for the dusting of petroglyphs on high canyon walls — the buffalo owned the land and by their grace shared it with two-legged brothers and sisters. If a white buffalo moved with the herd, she came from the North, carrying prayers on her shoulders. It was an honor to walk with her, to sort her breath from your own, the white edges of her eyes, the thick white coils of her mantle, the soft white hairs of her belly. She carried the voices of the gods, brought snow to rest the land, brought out of the red rock tender shoots from the lick of the wind, corn from the sun, and during those seasons when she did not move with the herds, she whispered her stories on the wind to carry for new generations of the animal-man, but when man took and took more without thanks, without reverence, the white buffalo was seen less and the people were not strong enough, savage enough, to protect the herds; and the thunder of hooves, the hard dance-points against packed earth began to diminish; the voices of the gods no longer carried on westerlies, no longer heaped on the wise shoulderbones of the elders, were not passed to strong youth, and the song of the buffalo was lost to the plains, and the pale men who began to spread like butter over the land of the buffalo could not see the spaces no longer filled by musk and whispered stories, did not know that the loss of nations hung in the air.

SQUADRONS

They come in formation,
pointed into the wind,
parallel to the beach.

It's early fall, late for maneuvers,
their shapes vary, reforming
the wedge.

Fog pours down the beach cliffs,
tunnels into each crack and cranny.

Out of the gray they come,
their great dark shapes nothing more
than shadows without edges.

>   Over England
>   they came in darkness,
>   flew past before the rumble
>   of engines, before the bomb bays
>   opened, the cross-hairs aligned.

Still they come, materialized
out of fog, a silent vee
equal distance wing to tip.

They glide lower, close to the
water, an easy guide along the sand
Different bombers, these search

for different targets, and breaking rank
turn their beaks toward water
and plunge after fish.

REGARDING BUGS

The paper tells us the Japanese love
bugs but the market has dropped.
Stag beetles used to cost thousands of yen,
Goliath beetles even more, and their accessories:
mossy branches, delicate bamboo cages,
shining beetles, cozened and coddled.

I too, am a lover of bugs, their shiny carapaces,
intricate joinings, the reverse bends of their legs,
the fantasy horns, hooks, the menacing,
efficient jaws, and their determination.

I have lain full on an oak leafed hill and watched
a caterpillar work its flurry-footed way on a path
that seems to have destination—its plush back
rising and falling over uneven grade
like a luxury car with good suspension.

I watch them meet—two furries—palpate heads
and bodies before passing on their ways, or
meeting another species, the palps touching,
the bodies pulling back in sudden reconsideration,
the decision to avoid, retreat, turn aside.

I have watched a dung beetle work its trophy
across a rutted trail, pushing with conviction
up the high wall of a boot print, tumbling back,
trying again. Robert Bruce's spider has nothing
on my dung beetle. We meet on this
muddy path, she with her great persistence,
I with admiration and a reluctance to leave her
on her own, for there are birds here,
and she is fixed on workload,
has forgotten vigilance, and we have been
well-met on this path, and I have loved her.

WINTER BEARS

In the basement where bears live
is an open river to the north
where we must go.
Bears pace in ovals, rumble
on slickered pads to the rhythm
of wood feathers, seeds that
bloom in quick-step along our path.
We follow the spoor of great elks,
web-hung with mistletoe,
their feet in delicate leaf points;
and badger scat, his wide stripes
furrowed ahead of us, leading north
where we will go, where the lines
line up with white, and 300 words
for snow. The bears stir
in a bear dance of winter coming;
they trek for caves where seasons slow
and the woofle of deep reversible sleep
keeps time with chains of inner earth.
There in the north, *the wise one*
holds aloft her icicled fingers,
five-sided paw prints to mark a borealis
and the bears, rustling fur to fur,
wend steadfastly up the map, counting
the latitudes of their going.
I puff out my breath, harmonic to their throaty
g r r r r.
As we go they tell me of last April
when they woke to blazed greening
and air charged with equinox.
How they paused at the cave to gather

their heartbeats, sleek their coats,
with a dreadful emptiness insistent on forage.
They had slept all those white months
in the haunches of *the wise one.*
Again we move toward that pool
of charmed bear, compelled by sleep
and the lowering of heads, fur-curled
together in dens of this season.
Legs, the broad ridges of backs,
thick necks, their ears round as clam shells
cocked for winds from the north
and their nostrils bold.
I would crawl into their furnaces,
slip among cilia to the brain of bear
to curl in their secrets
and leach out their myths,
so by this thirst I could become them,
bears heading north where the cave
haunts each season, sinking its message
into berry and fish that the curve of claw
has enfolded this year, pulling out
the long string of winter to come
and the bears unblinking, my two-legged stride,
my furless parchment naked and chilled.
Their great neck humps shake down
the long spines of musked pelt;
shift a little to load me in
to the center of their navigation where I breathe
the cumulus of brown fur, prickling my cheeks
as we match strides, ever north
toward the white horses — toward

a cave where we'll rest in a circle,
these bears holding back their teeth.
Their claws click on granite and dried oak leaves,
on a path no one sees, on the path pulling north
toward the end of the day, toward a cave
full of fur clumps and powdery lost bones
where the dust floor has hollows
that call to night-bears who are weary
of trails and ready to slumber,
their dreams on their shoulders.
We have followed the scent lines, heard
the crow rasp overhead, smells of autumn
are behind us decaying into spring
and the hoary dried smell of ice hangs low,
still pulling us toward that high shelf
where nightmares linger
and the stars are curtained.

One Bird Falling

A bird falls,
spinning in widening circles,
like a spiral losing its tension,
or a pebble dropped in a pond.
The bird is already lost,
some distant shot, or a falcon
pierced then let it slip, and it falls
pulling the sky after it.
Like eggshells collecting again
in a film run backwards.
The waters of the pond reflect its coming.
The waters of the pond open
like a passage and welcome the bird in.
Not a bird now, but a flutter
of loosened feathers, a pirouette
adrift on a pewter eye.
No one can put this bird back together.
No one can uncrack the egg
of this world. The heart
flutters against itself. The bird,
which has fallen into the water
has sunk from sight, feathers have drifted
and spilled over the distant weir.
The rift closes over itself
and the surface, again, is smooth.

AT THE DENTIST'S,
OPENING NATIONAL GEOGRAPHIC
TO A DIFFERENT PAGE

In tropical forests
ornithologists
spread air nets
to capture birds
and let them go altered
with ID bracelets. I wonder
if they exchange them
in the canopies
as we did in seventh grade
a new part of their mating ritual,
and the scientists
full of faith in metal and numbers
base their studies
on the belief
that birds are faithful
to theory.

A Cloud of Bats

Sitting by the campfire at Lake Tahoe,
bats begin to soar and sweep
overhead, black fingers against
the darkening twilight.

Not like the cave in Costa Rica,
where the mouth opaqued as bats
went sonar in a cloud so thick
you couldn't distinguish wing
from wing.

Naughty boys think it's fun to
throw a cherry bomb into a bat cave.
Lovely loud bang, lots of dead bats;
even more bats die because their
sonars are destroyed.
And now, white nose plague
threatens the rest.

Who will pollinate their bat flowers then?

BEARS

in the never quite blackness of night,
bound through star-fields
eluding Orion's sheathed sword.
Ursus and arctos, bjorn, ourse, and oso
guided whalers who would sweep the seas.
Gave breath to navigators in small
hand-hewn barks.
Dipping paddles into the barm,
man bore the secrets of old ways
to a new coast, where bears,
with a haste born of instinct
teach fishing to their brown-hued cubs.

THE BEETLE

She was small, and blond,
wearing a pink shirt
and well washed jeans.
Her flat hair hung over one eye,
as she bent to study
a yellow spotted beetle plowing the grass,
next to the sidewalk.
Mommy, why does the bug have so many legs?

It needs them to walk.

But I can walk with two legs,
and look, I can go faster.

Ah, said her mother,
but the intricate journeys
and errands of beetles require
many tiny legs.

A STORM OF FEATHERS OR SUDDENLY, FEATHERS

The air is full of feathers,
thick with them, drifting, falling,
                              feathers,
meandering down, floating up. They land
like snow on wave and branch. It's difficult
to see mountains. Difficult to see
rooftops and jungle gyms.
                              Feathers
are multiplying, some invocation of the wind
calls them. A blizzard
of feathers. The children run out
and catch them on their hands. I run out.
The dog barks in confusion
and delight. Give us this day.
                              Give us these feathers.
Give us back the birds that wore them.
Examine the fine veinery, the hollowness
of their spines, the nib points of their hold fasts.
                              Feathers
primed with air gather in clouds of white,
of color. The Earth clothed in them.
The great oceans are clogged with them.
                              Feathers
are become the Earth. There is no place
without them. The ground is thickening
into a flood of feathers. No levees to hold
them. They rise against the trunks
and around back doors. They silt
the windows. We live in a bowl of
                              feathers.

Even the wind is corralled. Feathers are
all we see. They settle and shift.
Sound is muffled. Bird song is gone.
They have released their
                                    feathers
and moved off, looking for better weather,
better landing, open branches. We regret;
it's a dazzle; we repent; a mortuary
of feathers. We are sorry.
Come back, Jack, Come back, Jill
Come wing and beak, come trill and caw.

A Bug Encounters Nirvana

I scratch my arm
and blood pools slowly.
A dot of bug

makes of it a watering hole.
I shoo him repeatedly, but he is back,
dainty with his feet.

Impatient, I swat him
and he falls feet up, still.
I feel remorse. I swatted
annoyance and hit a living being
that had need of me.

Who knows what my small lake brought him,
moisture, salt
or how far he flew in search.
Was it necessity or luxury
that made him careless?

I could have spared him.
I had a choice.

Bolinas Lagoon

Out of marsh grass
seemingly empty
the white shawls
rise into air
and fly

Walking the Geography of Other Nations

At the outlet of the river, where water runs
cool and fresh into salt, its muscle flattens
into a low run at the waves,
like a single wolf will run crouched
and come in under the belly of danger.

We walked the littoral of Oliver Lagoon,
mud, like black bean soup up our shins
and it sucked at our boots, possessing.

The forest was quiet; skunk cabbage and devil's club
their huge leaves like a giant's garden,
one armed with odor, the other with thorns.

We followed bear paths, reading their stories:
here the cloven < < < of a deer going fast,
there a scatter of bones, then the flat shovel-dent
of bull moose hoof, his velvet caught
on the hemlock's torn bark.

Ho, Bear, we shouted as we walked his realm
stepping over evidence of fox and our first bear scat,
old now and dried into a tidy bundle of feathers.
And then — large paw prints. Something was coming in
under our bellies, something was a shadow in the spruce.

And rounding an elbow of path — green, wet, fresh,
bear scat still warm. The woods were full of eyes.
Ho, Bear we called again, this time in homage, in surrender
as we retraced our steps, yielding the forest.

THE GREATER SANDPLOVER

Yesterday, a bird showed up —
drifted down on a wind luff
and settled on the Bolinas sand — just a bird —
wings, anorexic legs, nondescript beak.

Alone and off course; meant for Africa
or central Asia it was all out of landmarks,
had somehow misplaced North
or was it time for South.

It poked its beak into the sand,
seemed oblivious to aloneness,
used to poking along shorelines,
it darted in and out of spume and current.

What then was its reaction as people began to gather,
bristling with binoculars, camera, and the
unfamiliar chatter of cell phones,
their feet pressed ever closer, numbers growing.

This bird, its homing skills seriously in doubt,
had landed on a beach perfectly good for food
but a feathered miracle for birdwatchers —
a life bird — a new count on their list.

And the birders — do they want it to remain,
to make the rare common and everyday?

THE DANCING BEAR

The dancing bear has no option
but to keep her feet moving.
She waves her paws
as she turns, awkward,
obedient, eyes dull as old cloth,
and struggles to remember.

She has done this performance
on countless nights,
fringed jerkin, red tassels,
those faces and clapping hands
that don't know about the insistence
of sun through thick leaves or how

spring streams build to thunder.
She remembers black berries
strained to plumpness, and how
claws she once had
could shinny up smooth trunks after honey.
A time when the urgency

of food gave thrust to the day
and no human voice was heard.
Does she remember taking the whip's
sting as she roars toward the slit
of daylight to *out there;*
when she thinks she could make it

past the grid and smell of towns,
blend like smoke among trees again.
But too many roads, too many
cages and the clicks of track
and wherever she looks,
there seems no forest left to enfold her.

FLIGHT FEATHER

The feather
with its hollow quill
barely heavier
than the air
it must move
must float
its bird body
on winds
and currents rising
off the land
up the mountain aretes
out into space
feather
that makes thousands
of horizontal wipes
a day
without breaking
that fragile tube.

SAINT FRANCIS PREACHES TO THE BIRDS
painting by Berlinghiere   13th century

In the tree, black birds
are lined in neat rows like a musical score, their
yellow arrows pointed west, and across the space
the saint overlaps in triplicate,

three bald pates, three fringes,
three scratchy robes with a sliver of white down the tie
where the sun catches something that isn't humble,
some flash against the vow of poverty,

a vow the birds know better
than to take, having nothing to do with the clatter
of gold and more to do with a lack of seeds
or too many gray mornings that seep beneath
their feathers and into bones, hollow and pliant.

They face the saint, expecting,
because he has worked his fame on kindness, on feeding,
so that rows of them have forgotten how to search
through the wheat and thistles for plump nuggets.

What does the triple Francis want
from the birds he bends toward, keeping his hands
at his multiple sides, no offer of open palm, no arms
out as welcoming branches. The birds remain
on their side of the paint and wait.

They're without curiosity
and he cares little for the pull of worm against beak,
the suck of earth that finally lets it go. Nor does he
examine the way a yellow eye swivels its black center
to take in its circumference, the least movement.

They look orderly on their branches,
a troop of good soldiers. They take his millet and give him
a reason to wander in worn sandals without toiling
in the fields. They're willing, the pay is good. Cold nights
go easier with full bellies.

Francis will wander with his placid smile
and they'll follow. Why not. His pockets have holes, the trail
is easy, and it looks good. These birds have given up their
maps to the grain fields, have forgotten their knowledge
of scarecrows.

Heads cocked, they wonder
if he accepts the droppings that spatter his cassock,
or doesn't he notice, one of the prices paid for a life
of dusty paths and the empty bowl at his waist waiting
for some non-saint to fill it.

He'll beseech sacks of grain
from farmers, showing them the trailing flocks,
the tined prints. What farmer would turn his back
on God's anointed, take a chance on lightning
and the twisting winds that carry away fields.

AT THE WINDOW

A bird
believing in the sky
flew like a muffled drum
into my window.

I worked my way
around the roof edge
to the body, stiff
and gloriously yellow.

The eyes were veiled
but the beak opened
and closed

creaky hinge
and the hollow chest
clicked its uneven breath.

For half an hour
I cupped it in my hands,
while it gathered strength

and when it struggled
with equilibrium
I placed it on its feet
on a roof bulge

where it hunched
and blinked
readjusting to air.

It battled its wings
against openness
to gauge if it was
what it knew.

And finally,
composed
it flew on the wind
like a yellow blossom
to the long limb of the pine.

SACRED SPOTS

Pampas grass blowing
like prayer flags.
Tree trunks gnarled
and a glacial erratic
rooted in the meadow.
A fence of telephone poles,
solid, rounded, leaning
a bit askew from years of weather,
casting their shadows moving
as the sun rounds the sky.

And the white god,
neck crooked, legs tucked under,
flashes up from the estuary
reaching for its quadrant of sky.

NIGHT BEAR

She-bear in my shadowed valley,
rides out the nights with her shoulders
burly and her thick rump.

She comes with ghosts of goddesses,
their handmaiden, their hunter-companion.
Alongside the great warrior, Diana,
she rides the night sky
slipping along the edges of sleep
like a bushel of wheat needing to be sorted.

Resurrection from long winter quiet,
the deep rumble of her engine slowed.
She germinates like the rhizomes in my garden
waiting for the pull of seasons —

and while she slumbers, the sperm of her mating,
the eggs of her body, swim within her
kept apart by some hibernal tide that says
not yet, so that the birthing time
and the waking time come as one

and so she leads me from one life to
this present one, circles turning
to a new place, carries me forward
as she does her cubs, hidden but alert.

I am of her tribe and our scents
mingle at night
on the equinox breeze.

Cat Who Says No to Schroedinger

Cat in a box with a vile vial,
in the dark without even a peephole
for company; no large brown orb
peering in at a cat in the dark who
wants out. Unleashing his bionic
claw, his well-honed teeth;
he enlarges a hole, leaving behind
the acid, the atom and a few tufts
of black hair. Another near miss,
still eight lives in his pocket.

Cat with No Need of a Fiddle

Moon full of cream
lights his softpadding feet. Cat
without ukulele
walks up moonbeams,
inserts a bendystraw into Mare
Fecunditatis and sucks out milk
until the moon is reduced to a croissant
and so he eats that as well.

Cows

Cows,
pastoral, pacific, cud-chewing,
hillsides of cows
with their endless methane burps.
Guernsey, Holstein, Galloway, Dexter.
Like Ferdinand, they bury noses
in cowslip, clover, and buttercup,
nibble the sweet grass to
brownness, consume our prairies,
eat farmlands of corn,
Ayrshire, Kerry, Jersey, Brown Swiss.
Their calves may spend short lives
suspended in crates.
Many are harvested
anonymous as apples,
fed into the maze
that leads to the abattoir.
Red Poll, Shorthorn, Milking Devon.
4-H kids, for so much a pound, sell
their pets into rump steak
on the fall of a hammer.
And yet, in the land of Heidi,
a Queen Cow
sports her garland of flowers
and the biggest bell
as befits her rank,
leads her sisters to high pastures
as she has since the mountains were young.

KENJI

brings me presents
that hurt my heart.
Broken mice
he flings past my knees
in widening arcs, catching
the still softness
on the tips of his claws
like Willy Mays in center field.

Delicate birds,
their chests frantic with fright,
feathers spread across the room,

a series of garter snakes
feigning death on Turkish rugs
and yesterday, a lizard
stretched just out of reach
behind the piano.

I tell him
he's a good fellow
for doing what he must.
And if it's dead,
I let him play with it.
After all, he's been encouraged
by store bought toys
and instincts he was born with.

But if they live,
I cannot turn my back,
get out the dust pan,
or a bucket for the snakes

which come to life in sinuous eights,
stretch three fourths their length
up the pail, almost out.

I take them to a safe place
where leaves and vines give shade
and shelter, at least for now.
I tell them,
Avoid this place —
a cat lives here
who knows his business.

WHAT ABOUT COWS?

Horses revert to wildness, run free
as antelope across the bucking plains.
Cats turn feral; dogs
in close-flanked packs howl on the scent.

But cows we've gentled into stuffed animals
full of milk, brown eyes and metronome tails.
They stand endlessly inward,
lie down before rain.

SEASON OF THE CRANE FLIES

It's that time of year
when crane flies arise
for their brief season in the sun
and in our house.

Long legged and fairy light,
they seem to strive
to get inside, gather at screen doors
and seize the slightest opening

to zip and take up residence.
I cup them and blow them outside
but often before I can close
the screen, they flit back in and settle.

Theirs is a short life,
I should be honored
they wish to spend it with me.

COYOTE SKULL

Wind blows
through the sockets of your eyeless skull
Once the pad-foot
of our midnight dreams
Ghost voyager Moon dog
Bone landscape of lost tricks

An Empty Shell

Shells lie half buried on the beach at Tortaguero.
Spiraled like a unicorn's horn, so many of them,
crisscrossed. I collect them, each so beautiful
like weathered ivory. Cast off by their owners,
or some storm, or too much sun. Empty.
The least wind ruffles thru each golden mean.

But this one, a little more heft, a little moisture,
and I see the tiny claw across the opening
like the portcullis at the Tower of London.

Some life has claimed this shell as home. I rest
the shell on my palm and wait. The warmth
of my skin causes the shell to wobble. The claw
begins to slowly undefend, moving out toward
the edge until it touches, so tentatively, my flesh.

What's this?
Slowly a small crab begins to unwind itself
from the unicorn shell, tiny legs unfold,
revealing feelers and eyes stalked like black beads.
What astonishing courage it must take to explore,
to venture onto alien land. Was it like this

for Neil Armstrong, terrain incognito?
The crab moves its cumbersome shell across my hand.
The shell is too long to control. The crab is too
exposed to keep balanced. It tiptoes toward the edge,
feels the drop that leads to the unknown.

A CLOWDER OF CATS

Once I went — dawn barely breaking —
to the Roman Forum to catch the early
shadows that seemed to make
a time machine of the place, and discovered
in nooks and crannies of history, hundreds
of cats curled against morning dew.

The Forum cats are famous, feral,
but not too proud to welcome
handouts from loyal daily cat lovers.

Our cats make a small clowder
on our bed each night, and on the
sofa, and in a patch of sun
by the window.

Not feral, unless you pat their soft
bellies, then — shazaam —
claws and teeth!

A Scuttle of Crabs

Sally Lightfoots, rampant
on the islands, bright red and yellow
and BIG. They clack, tiptoe across
the rocks in sidelong scurries.

Pebbles on an empty beach
suddenly rise on eight stiff claws
and blur across the sand, hunker low
then rise again and scuttle
sideways, their shadows following
like obedient servants, crouch again
as one. There is safety in numbers, I guess,
and gulls wheel above.

As I try to walk the shoreline,
it's an obstacle course, precision,
care, my big feet a menace. Can they
watch foot shadows and diving birds
at the same time.

At our home beach, hermit crabs
carry their borrowed shells as they
ventured over sea lettuce and
crusted rocks. I pick one up. It seems
empty, but look, a grate of claw
across the opening. On my hand
it tickles as it ventures this soft
strange surface, with edges
and a plunge.

How Fleeting Is Fame

When the cow jumped over the moon
I showed up just as she landed, shaken
loose of her milk and mightily pleased
with herself, wondering where the crowds
were, the reporters. After all, how often
does a mere bovine achieve trajectory —
summon the cow-ness to arc straight up
and over that false, reflecting orb.

She had planned it. October 18th
when the moon was fullest, and in the
darkness of early morning. All would depend
on a clear night and the happy smile of the sun,
out of sight but glowing against lunar surface.

The cow having spent weeks practicing leaps
in the far meadow, chewing on buttercups
for energy, climbed up the tallest hill, and
as she'd figured out geometry and geography
launched herself, haunches clenched, front
legs lifted like arrows, and leading with her nose.
She soared up, a heifer-bolt of pure lightning
up until she peaked above the Sea of Tranquility,
before rotating 180 and began the long
curve down, until, right before my startled eyes

she landed, front legs first, stood a little stunned
and then, as if it was easy as salt-lick,
she looked around, expecting a fuss and
what a debacle to find she must, through history,
share her triumph with a fiddle playing
cat and that silly dish and spoon.

NEW DOG

The dog rips into morning
his steel toes dancing
on my bare ones
like 20 little knives.
He's young as blueberries in spring
and eager.
The night has been long to him.
Light means play
and a romp on the hills.
He has no use for work,
listens for car engines
that take him along,
that bring home his beloveds,
the ones who stroke his velvety ears,
who top off the water
and fill the bowl,
the ones who reach for the leash.

WELL MET IN THE WOODS

The moon hangs low
as deer are caught against the red saucer
of its fullness, ears alert to silence,
and a fawn
still spotted, in the thicket
where its mother dropped it.

I plunge like a truck without direction,
not like the deer, patient hooves
placed close and noiseless on narrow paths
that criss-cross the mountain, paths so slim
you cannot see the break in the timothy
until you are upon it.

There are things I find on the trail, bone
from a small animal, hollow wing of the hawk,
flickered feather from the low swoop of an owl.

I don't find the bones of deer
but am often caught, surprised,
to look up and find them — still — watching me,
velvet on their antlers,
eyes large and pooled in brown.

Which of us is wild?

I welcome their loose freedom.
It keeps streets from seeming so dirty,
buildings close and so very rectangular.
It helps to narrate the woods,
knowing I am watched, what I imagine
to be curiosity in their tableau,

as if they hope I will not move, so they needn't
so they can siphon from me
the dimensions of my alien ways.

They seem patient, which I am not.
This is what they teach me, demonstrating
how to linger the moments
among dry leaves, the sky caught in thickets
of winter oak, insistent scrawl of a jay
who warns and warns again,

Be wary
their legs are not hollow like ours.
They don't rely on their own strength,
no antlers, no sharp hoof kicks, no long
necks to make teeth a weapon. They cheat
with metal, ride on things that go faster than
we can, and they catch us for sport, like flies,
like a slapped mosquito.

I am the one who cannot hold, who
moves first, only an adjustment of legs
but the spell snaps, the deer
turn their heads and move off slowly,
a fade-out in the last reel,
they join the trees,
become leaves and grasses,
become soundless and gone.

At Limantour Beach

The old dog celebrates.
Sniffs high. Races to the water
and runs a tight circle in the shallows,
two, three, and then another.
She lowers her shoulder
to an Irish green swatch of sea lettuce.
She will roll in it, if she can,
if we let her, and wear it
as a badge of this day.

A day she always dreams of, by the fire,
legs churning on the rug — a beach day.
She can never get enough. Every beach
is a another notch in her dreamtime.

She selects a rock, smoothed and oval,
carries it dangling from her mouth
like a talisman.
It is a digging rock. She drops it.
Chases it with her paws, poking her nose
in to scent its trail.
Her grey muzzle is thick with sand,
her legs, and around her eyes.
Her tongue is sandpaper, coarse grit.

By the third hole, she must sink to rest
every eight paw strokes, or so,
haunches perched on the slag of her own mining.

We spend the whole day at the beach,
marking the water's edge with a long line
of holes and heaps.
Tonight, while she runs
before the fire, the tide will rise
and replace all her divots.

GREEN

Green the dinosaurs, long necks waving,
uncertain in an early spring,
their gulpings of wet verge
slop from noisy mouths, and green
their eyes as they roll them 'round
the mountains, green even their toes,
the size of small bending trees curled
into the soft loam of flighty grass.
Green bubbles on the surface of a scum-pond,
algae cell-dividing faster
than the dinosaur can lower her ungainly neck
faster than she can scoop
her green organismic breakfast,
and green the ripples and frothings
and the croak-frogs, and treetops
that dinosaurs look down on, dribbling algae
and grass sprigs into tree hair.
As the earth goes *greenhouse,*
and meteors cut the atmosphere
to crash earth, crash air,
and turn it all away from green.

OFF THE TRAIL

The dogs are going crazy, running
in eddies around and around
circles getting wider

their heads and tails bobbing
against the sky — out of sight
back again.

The smaller dog's tail
long and tipped white
serves as a fish bobber

to show where the line of dogs
pays out against currents of wheat.

They bark and yap
in huge bursts of sunlight,
ground soft and green
under their pads.

There is something about dogs
loose as wind that lifts the heart
as they run, fling themselves
over hills and hummocks.

You forget about paths and long to follow
off the well-trod and into the whisper
of grasses practicing free verse.

The dogs are frenzied with all they must fit
into their moments, their necks free
of leashes, their legs given to whatever strides
they choose. They race so fast, with such

buck and canter, that a new smell
jerks them almost off their feet.

They poke their noses without caution,
drink it in as if it were brandy.

When have we last given way to smell,
lingered to draw it into the nose, let it run
warm as liqueur down all the senses of the body?

When has a smell been so grand
we have longed to roll in it,

as the black dog does now,
four legs flailing at air, tongue lolling,
head dancing side to side,

all the full-out running and leaping
abandoned to this?

TURQUOISE-FACED DRAGONFLY

One day, swimming straight out
from the shore of Tahoe, I came upon
a dragonfly floating. Its delicate tracery
of wings sodden and depleted.

I am one of those artists who recycle
such treasures and so, with one hand
paddling, I carry it back to my towel —
lay it out to dry, return to my book.

I've told this story before,
but it sticks like a bur,
a sort of water-death miracle,
how two hours later, life

returned in a flicker and increasing
movements and then, I did not see
it go, but some time that afternoon
as I baked on the sand, a dragonfly

over my head, circled and dived, circled
and dived. I took it to be a sentient
connection (my water-mate?)
checking in that all was well.

As in a Dream They Pass

They keep coming nose to tail
nose to tail down the river bed
Five abreast their flanks shift

as they walk big thighs
push the back legs up and out
and the front legs pace
steady as rain

down the river bed five abreast
they are marching to wherever the river goes
to meadows a cool drink
at the lip of a spring

On high ground I cannot see the source
the endless shine of late sun
on their racks fingers of bone jutting
to the cardinal points There is

a slow rhythm to their walk five abreast
heads held straight eyes
that do not vary from the step
from the poll of the head in front   Antlers

gliding above them a separate
landscape that happens to be going
in the same direction I feel naked
watching them pass those trees of bone

Where are they headed
with their trust of arroyos

If rain comes and the pounding of water
sounds over the hills will they hear
the call that marches them out of danger
or are they set on this dry cut

moving to a promise ahead a time of year
that pulls them downward Dun brown
dusty uniform hides that ripple

as legs keep up the pace Five abreast
their brown skins bone muzzles brown
river bed rocks waterless grass air
brown as the dust they raise

covering the sky and deep brown
like new chestnuts their eyes that never vary
never roll to the side maintaining always
the forward stare of the herd.

A MOMENT IN THE MARSH

gives time to walk
among the mossbanks
and converse with minnows

plying their watery trade
along a marshfield
hot with cloud-reflected scapes

wind, gentle as a spring dawn
ruffles the sea reeds
while fish, unmindful

of the egret's glittery eye
circle its legs
like some surprising Maypole

as we once did
we carefree girls
below the beak of God.

SHORT TALE OF THE ELEPHANT

The elephant eats everything,
excretes enough. He bloats
and burns, how he burns.
Nature's monster is a holy god
of Goa. You know him: one tusk,
and holding a book.

The elephant's child eats dreams,
see everything, learns to avoid
the poisonous bush, how to dip
his trunk below caked mud
to find water. Flaps
those large efficient fans.

He'll grow up with the boar
and incite the poet.
The touch of his tongue,
his papery trunk. He is curious,
and also curious, an accident
of flesh, aggregate of many bizarrities.

The elephant loves and masticates
in his paradise: eats, eats, eats
and avoids the beach. Lava like,
he's a moveable room. He plods.
Don't anger him, keep an accord.
Look out ants.

CATCHING FISH

Catch the liquescent fish
silvering their way up weir
and water trail. How they fickle left
and right, streamline around boulders,
soldier through a shallow rock garden.

I can winnow among them, let their
slipped notes brush around my fingers,
a minor obstacle of their shoving upstream.

I could straighten my knotted net,
cast its shadow cross-hatched through the sun,
gridding fish like a finished game of Battleships.
My net would catch them, a closed tunnel ripped
into their flying. The fish filling it blindly

would blunt their noses on entrapment,
hang limp as I lift the net, the last
of their water simpering off shining scales,
mouths agape, gills flailing in search
of what is unexpectedly not there.

In the open focus of sunlight
I am reluctant
to cull even one.
Those I might have snagged
are far upstream by now.
And as I hesitate, another pulse of fish
and another.

AND OF THE WHITE EGRET

And what of the white egret
broken on the woodpile,
against the musked dark of the wood.
Beak, neck, crookless now, hang
limp and elongated over the side.

It frightens the dogs, who take turns
exploring it, before backing off,
confused by its wild white quiet.
They bark, and then the black lab
howls.

The stillness of its wings
takes us back to last Friday,
when an egret posed
along a weir of incoming tide,
head cocked, alert for small fish
tickling its feet. Then,
we could not marshal our next step,
locked in the presence of a god.

GLIDING IN ON A RIVER OF STARS

A fox hangs out near the back barn,
occasional red flash you only think
you've seen because it can't be verified,
he's that quick. He's never
near the mid-barn though sometimes grass
is bent in a hollow that might fit his shape, and
certainly not the near-barn though the chicken
population fluctuates in an odd way. Still,
there's no way in, no holes dug
around the deep, stiff fence, no red fur
caught like sunset on barbed wire.

Boards of the hen house are freshly painted,
show no scrape of claw, no scrawl of teeth
and yet the hens go, without a single strangled squawk,
disappear when the moon is down and shadows
blend into dark.

The fox has marked his territory on our minds.
We sleep uneasy, don't trust the tongue and grooved walls,
the fence firm and gridded in 4 inch rectangles.
How does he slip through our dreams and into the
anxious roost of hens. What is the rooster doing
while his girls are harvested? Does he blackmail
his harem into affection, *My Dears, I know a fox.*
The choice should not be hard...

LONGEST LEAP OUTSIDE CALAVERAS

Poor frog, split gut to nose, intestines uncontained,
    a population of eggs swarms like amoebae
    across the lab tray. Donnie turns greener than the late frog,
    slides delicately beneath the table.

We work that frog for a full week, less grid, less recognizable.
    I talk through each step. Donnie keeps his eyes squeezed shut,
    takes shallow breaths against the formaldehyde making him
    woozier than those lost eggs.

One morning, we learn to pinch nerve bundles running
    along the spine, and both legs flex at the knee like a ballerina.
    Donnie, who has finally parted one eye in a sloe-eyed slit,
    jumps as if he's been gaffed, lab tray takes flight
    and My Lady Frog makes her last prodigious leap

to a place of authority — Dr. McAusland's desk.
Detention for a week — both of us.

THE FROG WHO LOST HIS PIGMENT

And then, the frog who had lost his pigment hopped from lily pad to pad to see if he could find it hanging loose in the water. Quite excited, he thought it was just ahead, but when he got there it was a small pool of oil that discolored the water and not the celadon green he was missing. He asked the water skater if she had seen it. The water skater had been darting over the pond all morning, her wire-thin legs barely denting the surface, but she had seen nothing unusual. *My goodness, Frog, you look quite peculiar in your paleness. I wish I could help you. Try the coot, she's been nosing the rushes. Your pigment may have floated in and snagged there. But the coot, almost too busy to interrupt herself, declared she poked her bill into crevice and corner and she would certainly know if she'd seen loose green pigment floating around. What's more, Frog, wouldn't my beautiful orange bill be a sickly green if I'd been dabbling in your lost color. How did you lose it anyway. Seems rather an unlikely thing to do. Doubt if your mother would be pleased. I knew her you know, very ladylike, kept her bobbing and leaping to a cadence you might emulate...so graceful...a slight tensing and she'd lift off... such a parabola...legs trailing behind and hauled in just in time for landing. Not like you, Frog, you are extremely non-aerodynamic. You bunch yourself up like a lettuce-head and fling yourself at the sun. It won't do at all. Once launched, you seem to boogie in the air, your legs akimbo and waving at opposite horizons. I imagine you flung yourself right out of your precious pigment. I'd look upward if I were you.*

FIREFLIES

In the dusks of June, fireflies
rose like bubbles out of the grass
into the lengthening shadows.

We stayed up late
to welcome them to awl-punched jars,
the mystery of their sudden spark
that seemed to be *there, there, there*
our high delirious voices,
our pinafores like soft pink lights
flitting but not glowing.

In Osaka, families went out
across the fields on firefly nights
with their muted lanterns
and their soft punctuations of merriment,

and unseen until they arrived: a trench,
what we'd call a shallow arroyo.
It did not so much appear as glow,
like being in a night-plane
and watching cities nearing from the distance,

and when they looked in,
the trench was flooded with fireflies,
some spontaneous magic
caught in the empty web of night.

The Outer Beach

Like telephone poles in open country,
twelve fishers of bluefin stand angled
along the outer beach. Casting and reeling.
Casting again.

Beyond the waveline, fish
are running parallel to shore
and the strikes begin,
rods kneeling toward breaking waves,
the heel of each rod snug in the twelve crotches.
Winding, winding in the fish
riding surprised through water
until it feels the rising shore —
then it fights, leaps and thrashes
as it's pulled up the beach,
caught in unfamiliar air,
flopping and flipping
to get back where buoyancy counts.

This is catch and release.
I can almost live with it.
The triple hook pried loose
from the bloodied mouth.
Desperate fish, its only salvation
water.

The hook is loose before the next wave
almost reaches. The fish, sensing it,
arcs left, right, the next wave closer
and then the rescue wave,
humped and breathing froth,
lifting the fish and his terrible mouth,
taking him back.

COPPER FLASH

Oh frabjous fox
with your fur turned to fire
as you crest the ridge
on such a day.
Long tail rippled behind,
nose full to the scent,
liquid you are.

Oh farmer,
can you talk "fox" —
grudder, snork.
Can you tell him this bird
of all birds
is not his to claim?

Or is it a matter
of whose vixen and kits
need the chicken more —
you with your full flock
or he whose dens
you have plowed under
through years of ribbing meadows
that now grow tassels of corn?

His night scream
makes your finger itch.
Tip your hat instead
that he still persists out there
in what we've left him.

Frogs and Geraniums

Under the geranium pot,
in pebbles kept moist by watering,
lived a colony of frogs most people
never knew were there.

Each time I lifted the pot,
they rearranged themselves,
organizing their social order
like a quadrille.

I disturbed them too often
and they gave up their ceramic
palace and went elsewhere
away from human pests, but
the geraniums remained,
perky red
above the blue pot,
over moist pebbles and saucer.

The geraniums began to look tired.
They continued to put out blossoms
which no sooner opened, then faded
and leaves took on a curl that spelled doom.

The geraniums were not mine,
rather they were in concert with frogs
who in return for darkness and regular wettings
provided careful conversation that geraniums
found impossible to ignore.

They had flourished
above the underbelly of frogdom,
and thrown their proud flamenco heads
up with pride and conviction.

TURNABOUT BEING FAIR PLAY

Somewhere a fox,
glorious with setting sun,
walks slowly along the river bank,
stretches to the full height
of his hind legs
and shows off —
to the envy of his vixen —
his stylish trench coat
made of the supple stomach pelts
of 42 American women.

A CLOUD OF GRASSHOPPERS

Walking through a sun-baked meadow,
wildflowers gone to beige stalks,
the grass sparse and reedy, was it
the shadow of my footsteps, or the
vibrations of my tread that turned
the meadow into clouds of grasshoppers,
spronging every which way, to land
and fling themselves again?

Then quiet, then their back legs,
then the vibrato of their music
filling the air with sun, heat, dust,
grasses, and their *I Am Here.*

Like my son's guitar when he used
to sit in the sun at Tahoe and strum
out his song for all the girls to hear.

LOYALTY

A grey goose circles in a gray dawn,
round and round, honking softly. His mate
lies spread on the meadow below. No longer
moving — soon a feast for a fox — but the gander
remains for days before finally heading south.

Reminds me of the goose in the news photo
that fell in love with a rural mailbox and
refused to let anyone near his beloved.
The postman refused to service the box and the
owners tried, without success, to move it along.

The goose was faithful to the mailbox
even after someone knocked it over.
Alas the affair ended when someone shot the goose.

What are the degrees of loyalty. And when
does circumstance end it? The dog that lies
by the altar where his master once lay, or
the dog left behind by a traveling family,
that sat by the road for three years, looking
and waiting, waiting, and looking only to the right
where his car had disappeared.

Dogs understand the great attachment.
It's what we love about them.

SIX HORSES

Six tan horses ring the tub of water like spokes of a wheel. They face in, their muzzles deep in the cooling. They are covered with dust from the fields, & when they hear water gushing into the trough, they come....six direct lines.... pacing off the grass to get to water. They do not come together. They are not together in the field. They come from where they are when they hear the water plash against corrugated tin. Pick their heads up from the grass, pulling a last blade. Their ears prick forward toward the sound. They walk like ripples on a pond reversing. They walk toward water. Their nostrils flare as they smell it. They are thirsty & the water is ready. They walk. Ripples of horses coalescing back toward the place where the stone fell into the river. The stone is the bucket. The river is the sweet taste of fresh water. The horses are the ripples gathering again into the splash. The horses draw closer together as they center. The tub is slippery & wet. Water has sloshed over the rim & wetted the nearby dust. The hooves of the horses are dainty as they approach. They come as close as they can. They could, if they stretched out their necks only a little, touch noses, but they don't. They don't look at one another. Their brown eyes look down. Their necks lower long faces to the water. Their manes hang like curtains. Their withers twitch & calm again. The horses stretch their mouths. They feel the first touch of it. This is what they've come for. They plunge in nearly to their eyes. They drink long & deep. They whiffle air out of their submerged nostrils. This is their song.

WATCHER

I'm a watcher of hawks
how they cartwheel through curls of air,
how they ride the smooth waves
across the belly of the sky, soar
away from water, prefer Earth under their wings,
how the rhythm of their flying is supported by thermals
how they fly higher into their blue oceans
to reach those currents that cross inlets,
whales below, each unaware of the other;
unaware that below is whale, above hawk.

What they do not see, deep within they know,
each feels the rhythm of the other.
Sleek feathered hawk carried high in circles of blue,
and below, compressed by the weight of waves,
the great behemoth is easy in her belly, though
water is pulled off Earth, pulled by the moon,
as the whale is pulled north on a curl of the map

There are none like them.
Hawk, Leviathan keeping to their blue —
The hand of the wind extends to the hawk,
the cup of ocean expands for the whale.

HORSEBREAK CORRAL

This is where they tame them
to the saddle, the rein, the hard
metal bit and clank of snaffle.

This is where they lose their sense
of tribe, their feral love of wind.

Here they trade the high sweet clover
for oats, the fresh moving Skeander —
for a trough filled twice a week —
surface scum remixed.

Here their feet are shod
for the cold, rigid, pavement.

And here they are reduced to gaits
with proper leads. Instead of walk,

lope and full-out they are gentled
to this cadence of the ring

where they are schooled,
ridden: gee-ed and haw-ed.

What do they remember?

A Hummingbird's Heart
Beats 1400 Times a Minute

The symphony of a hummingbird
is all percussion and woodwinds.
The small heart drumming out minutes
in hundreds of beats
                and those tiny improbably wings
creating an oboe's notes in the wind.
I put out the fake petals, the engorged red
globe of sugared water — and wait for visitors.
              When least expected,
they swoop in and hover, deciding,
then beating out a song of flower and food,
unfurl those siphoning tongues and drink,
so fast I miss it all,
              see only the red flutter
of chest, rapid blur of wing beats,
then they dart away to the apple tree,
make those improbable little clicks
to each other. It's the clicks that usually
alert me.
              I stand still and wait
for that darting strike, the bomber-bird
coming in at a slant, fast and sure.
It stops dead in air, assessing source
and safety.
              I move not a muscle
and it glides in to drink, flitting this way
and that, little helicopter-bird
taking a chance on red.

RUNNING HORSE

shadow of others behind it
rush of speed,
wild energy racing
simply to be running.
Front legs reach forward
this is a wild flight with the wind
back legs pushing off
the blur of skin and fur
the thrust of muscle
flying mane as the horse
creates its own wind
its own path
there in the midst
of all the others.

Hawk Soaring

Man, with his black rimmed eyes,
glints at me from the tallest hill,
thinks he knows me, feels we are brothers
as he studies my habits, my feathered patterns,
but for him, airborne is just a three foot leap.

Over at Stinson playing Icarus,
they strap on huge metal frames, harnessed
to their jellied bodies. They launch
themselves in *my* sky, usurp *my* thermals
and drift in tightening circles, until gravity
brings them to a sandy landfall.
They cannot soar or carve the air.
Nor glide for distance, for they cannot
lift themselves to return.

I see them craned back, watching me tilt
at wind drafts and I give them
a good show, pullout all my tricks.
How I am washed by their envy.

If I Were a Horse

you could try, but could not
tame me. You could beat me
or whisper

> but I would be made of wind
> and long strides

not for reins and girths

> but for hills
> valleys for the fording
> of rivers rolling in new
> spring clover
> for running
> whipped by tall wheat

Not for me the corral or the sugar lump.
Don't braid my mane or tail,

> they are wind gauges
> my telltales

Don't give me a stall and blanket. I might
become used to them.

> give me open land
> with apple trees

No bit, no jangle of chains.
No metal bar between my teeth ripping
into my soft mouth.

                    give me spring and summer
                and I can make it through winter
                        coat grown shaggy
                         hooves padded

Not for me the jodhpur girl going *cluck cluck*
and *giddyap*. Not for me the spur or whip.

                    I know when it's time to run
                    time to roll on my back
                            I know
            where the rivers move into shallows
                    for a drinking pool

                leave my tail long and loose
                    it takes care of the flies

Don't hedge me with fences.
I want no neighborhoods.

            give me open space other animals
                    other territories
                give me shoeless feet
                    running room
                        bucking room
                    room to twist
                whinny at the sky
            let me snort in the dust

I don't need your leathered hand, your
oat bag, your curry comb.

                        I can curry
                     on a tree trunk
                  I can graze oats from the
                          source

Step back
and let me go

                     with the wind
                  with the scent of pines
                  out and out I go
                              and onward

IGGY

To Gill from Akumal

What I need to tell you is,
he's gone. After you left,
your bags stuffed with frilly dresses
for your granddaughters, after you,
one last time, looked thru your binoculars
at him looking statue-still at you.
After the door clicked shut
and the car started over the coral cobbles,
he bobbed his head vigorously up,
down, up, turned his impressive profile
and trudged west along the rocks.
We have not seen him since.

Perhaps he fell in some kind of love
with your raspberry shirt,
or your silhouette as you sat
on the walk-steps and watched him,
the bobbing of his head not
a warning but a salute.

It is warmer today. The wind
does not carry the cutting edge
of last week. His favorite rock
is full of sun, but empty.
Did he find the hibiscus blossoms
you put near his retreat
as a way of connection? Certainly,
they were gone this morning:
him or the wind.

I am sorry to report his absence:
the thick head, the camouflaged
scaly body, strong thighs over
rather delicate feet, the faded white
stripes along his spine ridge
and the last of him, seen
disappearing behind the seagrapes —
his long undulant drag of tail.

Considering Endless Night

When I was a child, after I'd turned off the flashlight,
I'd try to imagine what endless night would be,
that after the certain number of hours,
no dome of sun would appear to break open the horizon,
no long strobes of light would search
for trees and rooftops. I knew little then
about creatures who prefer the night,
nor those of deep sea trenches who depend on dark.

At the aquarium,
I stood in a room round with jellyfish,
silently pulsing, drifting in starclouds of plankton,
unconcerned by unaccustomed light.
It didn't help them avoid each other, rather
they glided through their liquid world,
bumping, nudging, caught and carrying,
as if blind, as if whatever they touched
was *there* — nothing more.

Their gauzy openwork parachutes
with which they make the world's longest migration
and do it nightly, rising
2000 feet to feed at the surface,
falling before dawn to their mid-sea existence.
Never to see the light, or each other's waltzing,
their long lovely trains drifting behind
like the finest Belgian lace.

PIECES OF CONSCIENCE

When the air still carried the cool of night,
my grandmother would declare carnage
on the beautiful Japanese beetles
that orgied through her roses,
and morning glories
whose pale blue bowls climbed the fence.

Take this, she'd say, handing me
a mayonnaise jar
half full of soapy water. Bubbles
fell over themselves to the jar's lip.

I had to hold it carefully;
it was heavy and slippery.
*Get as many as you can. Ugh, I
hate them.* And her kindly face
would twist. Outside,

the beetles were about their business
of eating. Where had they come from?
Somehow they knew my grandmother's roses
were opening. They were everywhere,
shards of stained glass, hindwings
carefully folded under hard brown forewings,
bodies glowing green as emeralds
hidden in a matrix of petals.

Each time I dropped the next one in
I saw how they climbed on each other,
slid on the glass sides, how their legs
spun them in circles and finally,
tired, poisoned, sodden,
their bodies dulled and sank to the bottom.

Birds didn't want them.
It was up to me, her reluctant mercenary,
to pick them off, polished gemstones
with six spiky legs, and drop them
in soapy water, where they died,
and I watched, a killer of creatures
too small to resist.

SCRUB JAY

Saucy jay, strutting on the railing,
patchworked with God's best blues.
He preens, puffs, turns to be sure
the world gets his best side, which as he knows
is all sides.

Near me, the cat appreciates; body tensed
forward, eyes locked, chin quivering
with guttural static — *ch ch ch ch ch* —
and the jay welcomes this safe attention.

Keeping watch, faithful as an old dog,
he sets his raucous warning into moments of calm,
flies in and out of the pyracantha with bits
of twig, pleased with offerings of cat fur
from groomings, chatters expansively
about bringing up his children.

He can be mean
as an old man who lives lonely;
querulous chickadees have been warned off,
clots of nest are whipped from the juniper,
the finches will have to begin elsewhere,

and yet I love
his gutsy solution to the suet basket
hung facing down, laced with insects
of the right sort to lure nuthatches.
Like a mockingbird, the jay
becomes another, perches on a lower branch
peering up at his treasure swaying seductively.

I see his mind and muscles tense,
then he launches his heavy body up.

For the necessary seconds it takes
to spear a beakfull, he is
a hummingbird, beating his wings faster
than any instinct instructs him, as he
hovers in place — a rich blue flash.

Birth of a Kestrel

In here is nothing
but the beat of my heart.
Around me a cage of bone
shifting from black to light gray.
I press it on all sides
until I can no longer move.

My beak takes up the beat, pick pick,
until a ragged line appears,
and spreads, and what is not
darkness slams against me.

I peck harder, and thin bone
parts into room to move,
into spreading my wings.
I push with my legs, forcing
my head through.

Something almost tears it off,
blows my feathers dry.
The bone walls break away and I fall
against sharp round things.

There are other feathers here
and two feet. There's
a huge beak pushing at me.
And there are

shapes reaching up: mountains,
and columns stretching down: trees,
and soon I will learn the winds that lift,
the thermals that will hold.

A School of Koi, Pausing

Shanghai, overrun with people
like a speeded up crowd in a movie.
Bicycles and wooden carts piled
unimaginably high. A man peddling,

pulled a bamboo wagon, on which
balanced a love seat, and on the
love seat, a sheep chewing pleasantly
in rhythm to the wheels. You couldn't

cross the streets. You couldn't maneuver
the sidewalks. Women pushed rattling
cages full of toddlers. Along the Strand
next to the little park that used to say

No Dogs or Chinese, the people pressed
against us, wanting to practice their English,
wanting to show off their one child splendid
in fine clothes. Soon we were at the old city,

streets winding so tightly the crowds must
thin to trickles of legs. We wound here
and there trying to keep track of how
to get back, until we came, breathless,

to the central square where the temple-house
stood and in front of it a wide garden pond
brimming with koi, a Shanghai of koi,
teeming and jostling. We stopped, leaned

on a bridge rail and watched the flutter of
fin and tail. Speckles of black and white
and red, some yellow. The koi were very large
and endlessly hungry. We bought small bags

of food and sprinkling some on the water
caused the entire population of koi to come
agitating and bumping right below us,
their white jawed mouths gaping open and shut,

sucking in the dissolving flakes as if it were
something precious and new. It was a small
pocket of peace, there in the middle of the most
populous city on earth. The bustle

of human business was left behind and only
the bustle of fish disturbed the surface.

An Exaltation of Larks

Morning comes washed
from last night's wind. Spring
air is clear and soft. Everywhere
my ears go, there are birds.
Not concerned with territory
but exclaiming the sway
of tree limbs, the sharing
of the season, and the joy
of wings

A Labor of Moles

It's not easy underground
without light, without
sight, digging tunnels, always
tunnels, side, slant, exit ramps,
a map held only in the head.

No pickax , no detonating,
no hardhat with lamp, no
gloves for our small pink feet.
Work, work and star-snouting
forward chewing on dirt.

Ice Wings

beautiful tragic weather —
an icefall
of sleeted monarchs

blizzard of color
avalanche of frozen bodies
bunched and huddled wings

caught in tropical downpour
and unprepared for frost
they were turned into delicate ice

in the millions upon millions,
entire crop of golden wings
nursery of generations

From trees, now empty hosts,
once festooned in orange & black
gorgeous curtains and furbelows

of monarchs are iced and cascaded
a foot deep on the forest floor
and still they plummet; sounds

of breaking ice against ice breaking
heaping the ground into foothills
an atlas of stained migration

ended before completing
the wild flurry of mating
Somewhere far north of here

each pupa spun
a translucent chrysalis developed
those lovely furled wings

emerged to warm them open
in the sun of our meadows and gardens
filled with mullioned orange

then heeding the season
they grouped in flocks
or determined singles

Reaching the cold windswept heights
they flew toward the tropical
nesting grounds of

Rosario Sierra Chincua — homeland
intuited in some collective archive
Usually the air so thick

no spaces showed between
wing tips overlapped
Trees shuddered

with their elegant burdens
air whistled with the beat
of wings in a montane forest

All reduced to this lumpy carpet
these transitory colors repaid in ice
where now of all the millions

only a few survivors flutter
back up to the high branches
desperate for sun.

CAMBALA ANNULATA

Millipede stretches her leggy length
along the apple branch like a breadstick
with a million poppy seeds. She skims
aphids from fruit flies, winnows the fattest,
traces their succulence with her pincers
and soon filled, dredges a path through the rest.
She palpates branch buds with her forward legs
as the other nine hundred shamble to keep up.
From high in the storm, a shrike scouts.
Millipede grovels at the rush of tight air,
swift-curls into a segmented knuckle and stills.
Shrike swoops low, pierces the sweetmeat and
ricochets overhead and away.

ORACLE BONES

On a piece of bone, a tusk,
is a story I can't read,
scratchings of a writer inscribing his saga,
little mousetracks of story, tiny bird feet
from the mind of a person unknown,
who spent inhospitable, sunless winters
committing him/herself to storyline.

Warming in my hand,
where it fits like a knife in its sheath,
I turn its pleasing shape
in slow, smooth increments,
drawing in those unknown letters
like breathing grains of pepper,
a slight irritant while they tangle their way inward.

I want to know what they say,
what they meant to the writer
with his sharp implement and careful hand.
Why he chose *these* words for his rounded bone.

Once I found the skeleton of a moose
along an unmarked path of my own devising.
Bleached by the sun to the palest parchment,
its femur an oracle bone
of those who had visited
as it decayed in heat and wind —
lapped by tongues, grooved by canines,
scribbled in the language of beetles —
intricate story of time passing,
tales to be read, these languages and epics
of the other.

A Parliament of Owls

In college, the endlessly fascinating
and frightening Dr. Patch
discussed Chaucer's owls, and
quite out of character, told a story
about his small grandson revealing
to the realtor, "There's an ow-ell
that lives in our attic."

Owls do not generally congregate,
not for discussion, not for the
enacting of laws. They are each
a parliament of the knowledge we
have assigned them, the souls
of the dead, the wisdom of the gods.

Of their own wisdom
we know precious little.

THE OWL IS A POEM

a flash of wings crossing the moon's
wash of light. What he hears
are the wires of small lives. What
he sees are stars of movement.
The owl lights the night

with his *whirrr* of passage. He flies
through gates of darkness,
withholding even his shadow,
yet the ground below shudders
and voles and rabbits

hunker and wait. Their paths
collide or not. The owl swoops,
talons flexed and shining.
Much depends on each catch.
The owl is a poem gliding,

silent, seeking the unwary,
the momentarily careless. His wings
unfurl like the sails of a boat in storm,
snapping open, held motionless
above the dampening grasses.

Across the meadow, the moon
lays its spill over the land, and the owl
keeps to the shadow-edge.
The moon is not a friend of owl.
The owl returns to the tree,

talons gripping the bark and dinner. He folds
his wings and calls softly into rising morning,
hoo hoo, sending his news
out to the neighborhood and listens, listens
for an answer, and she, too, is a poem.

LIKE A LITTLE LIGHTHOUSE
For Mary Oliver

I can see that owl
filled with its own satisfaction,
dinner fresh
off the snow chambers of open meadow,
how it has flown back
into protective cover,
swivels its head
sends out beams of light
from the Fresnel lenses of its eyes
        on   off
          on   off
sweeping woods and ground,
beak making sharp clicks
of expectation, shoulders steady as rock
and snug between balled claws and branch
the warm creature caught
before it could find shelter.
Life, death, life
as owl gains another day.

Perhaps it leans against rough bark,
mulls the keenness of its eyes
still able to catch the least movement;
somewhere in its brain give it a name,
one that means not snow, rock or sleeping mound
of river bank, but morsel
of the right size, right nourishment
and worth the flight, this exposure of owl
before dusk has fallen protectively
across the field
across the long wings
the speckled flash of speed.

Sounds are grounded, as if waves
could dash against its feet and still
it would hold,
the light would circle,
the glass steady,
the column still, and yet
this lighthouse of hollow bones,
with pinions like rudders, quivers
with awareness of what is smaller
swift weak
inattentive for one fatal moment
before the lighthouse unfolds its great wings,
explodes into the air
silent.

ORB WEAVER AND OCTOPUS
- Eight by Eight -

Radii of safe threads
crossed by the sticky spiral —
her operose weave is finished
for this moment
and she rests in the middle
of a many layered web,
each new facet as intricately spun
as the last: her silken oriel.

An ornament
in an ocean of air,
she waits motionless
for the oscillation which signals
the arrival of entrees.
Her long dancer's legs
thin as pencil lines,
ochre and black
with red leg warmers.

Below her, and below the wave rhythms,
water currents carry
to the shy and fluid octopus
an opulence of dinner.
Oars ovaled with suckers,
she's a shell needing no crew.

Orb weaver, gaudy, obtrusive,
sits center stage.
Octopus seeks obscurity,
preferring a slot in the rock
to hide from her wet world.
One sways in the air
the other lurks in the sea,
both depending on currents.
As do we. As do we.

A Romp, a Raft, of Otters

In the Tracy Fjord of Alaska,
great globs of kelp, no, look closer,
huge rafts of otters held together
by community. Babies or abalone on their
tummies, drifting, an indolent flap
of flipper.

But make a noise, even a slight one,
and they disappear as one, synchronized
swimmers with barely a ripple, which
moves toward you catching the sun.

PELICANS AT PYRAMID LAKE

beaks tucked close
white flock
gliding like wimples
over the stitched placid water

avocets and curlews
hidden by toad rush
quiet
only their strobe-movement
behind the grasses

on shore I am content
to suspend my thoughts
seeing residents, transients
of this lake
only as movement

now and then
a flash of color

AN OSTENTATION OF PEACOCKS

Once I worked at a nature preserve
where peacocks served as sentinels
and security alarms — they shrieked
with abandon like unoiled gates,
and flared their many-cyclopic tail-
feathers — preening and strutting
in slow staccatic circles

like that glamour-mad week of
opening nights: opera, ballet and
symphony, when the social
manikins don Armani, Blas, Chanel,
and strut sedately up marble steps
with their escorts as straight-men
and the other women as knives.

Glorious rustle of silk, shimmer
of velvet and satin; males reduced
to stick figures with bank accounts
and the women, unlike the peacock world,
taking the lead and rattling their tails.

You Don't Get it Unless I Crow

I am cock of the walk — all iridescence
and strut and I create the inky characters
of my story on the right side of the page
where I can peck at them if they become unruly.

I bring you the morning — up early,
while muezzins across this globe are checking
for the 3 white hairs on the black goat,
I open my throat to morning air

and haul up the sun like a fiery egg.
Too early for you? Tough luck, Old Sod,
time does not suspend itself for your lazy loaf.
Once Hokusai, took my brother, dipped

his feet in red sumi and let him run across
beautiful white paper, earning fame
for his maple leaves. Maybe I am that brother.
I'd like that kind of unrecognized fame.

I've made here the scatchings for man
and for heaven. I am between the two.
Higher than the man, but not quite
cocky enough for heaven. So I want

to ask you, If I don't crow and the sun
doesn't rise, what becomes of you,
smug-slug in your bed? Do you
creep about in the dark like the bean

pushers of the Navahos, seeking an opening
to the upper world? I have scratched out
a riddle, one you can only read in the light
I provide each morning, asking no praise...

it is enough I praise the morning, enough
that I hold the string, the doodle that pulls
the sun up out of the void, like a ball
sucked out of a swamp. Up it rises,

my glory, my responsibility. You, inflated
jerks, with your science, can explain
all you want. I crow. The sun comes up.
Ipso Facto. Plain as the nose on your sunlit face.

Crow. Sun. Shut me in the barn, I still crow.
Stuff your ears with cotton. The sun comes up.
Ergo, I crowed. Believe me, I take this
responsibility seriously even if you don't.

The silly muezzin over there, he can't count
goat hairs if I don't shout up the sun.
He knows this. Just won't admit it. Won't
credit me as he should. He's the one who goes up

the tower and tries to outcrow me with electronics,
with burbling and warbling, ululating, tremuloes.
Too bad. I've already crowed up the sun. Me —
Rooster. I'm the answer to the riddle.

I'm Cocky Locky. I'm Tom Riddle.
Read it and weep. How about an extra handful
of corn. Wouldn't hurt. Can't do anything about
the ozone hole, though. That's your job, dumb fuck.

Raptors

High on the thermals, raptors are winging.
They circle the heights, easing south.
      Buteos, Accipiters, Harriers, Peregrine

Red Tail hawk banks against clear air, flashing
the rufous under-blush that gives him name.
      Sharp-shins, Coopers, Merlins, Ferruginous

Their beaks are curved, their plumage concinate.
Slicing the wind, in sweeps the Kestrel,
sleek, small, and bullet straight. The Windfucker.
      klee klee klee   killy killy killy

Down in the canyons, raptors are circling
in long limousines. Executive-gray car phones
are riding the thermals of stock buys and leverage.
Sharp claws extended, they are wheeling the air paths,
and dealing down, and their beaks are red.
      sell sell sell   buy buy buy

In the deep dark of the penta-building,
raptors rip the flesh of war,
circle the heights of power, riding
thermals of their special interests.
Hawks tear the clean white dove feathers
into ribbons of red.
      rat-tat-tat rat-tat-tat

Deep in the dark undergrowths, the raptor is waiting.
His breathing circles, riding thermals of night,
in the parks, in the big, unweeded city.
His claws are curved, as he grabs, hurts, kills.
      And his cry is silence.

A Crash of Rhinoceroses

The ground shook with the aftershock:
skin to skin, horn to horn, bone
to bone. My ears rang with it.

Across the savannah, two rhinos
exercised their maleness in blunt force
trauma — head to head,

while the female serenely nibbled
nearby, at just-greening grasses.

Yesterday, still in Nairobi, I saw
two land rovers crash head to head,
clash of metal, screech of brakes and
breakage and one man flung out the door
was at rest on the white line.

I guess testosterone is built into all of them
and takes over common sense like a gale
through tall rushes.

The rhinos parted, snorted, and rushed
together again. The crash echoed from horizon
to horizon, and into the scrub brush
where the female had placidly wandered
to continue her dinner.

RIVERTRAIL

I see them clearly
beneath water Prussian blue
in the depths, a migration
of reindeer,
five abreast
walking the river trail
dignity keeping pace
with their high stepping hoofs.

Fully branched, their antlers point
beneath the surface
and haunch by haunch
the spots on their flanks glint
in the current,
water smooth over their heads.
Nothing seems to move but the river
and them in the river
they move and the river moves
and do not seem separable
one from the travels of the other.

At times, the racks of their antlers
breast the water, glide along
like branches cutting the surface,
languid ripples >>>> behind them.

I know these reindeer, am of them
somehow. I should be with them, moving
like myths off the tongues of elders
part of this wet inclusion. My hoofs
and my set eyes and the pommel
of my satined head
carry a proud rack
awkwardly
threatening my neck
with the newness of balance.

Rabbit. Who Could Hear the Stars

Once upon a tussock, Rabbit was considering the huge green cabbage that hangs in the night sky, so far away she can't distinguish the leaves that wrap the heart of the cabbage, the part she likes good-heavens-the-very-yes best. The night-cabbage had been nibbled away into darkness, and slowly this new one filled and grew and tonight was directly above her like the eye of a goddess, open, and bathing the rabbit with its celadon glow. The stars, which had covered the sky, pulled away from the cabbage, indignant each month as she raised her overblown self on high and overshadowed them with her pushy spotlight. They gathered in constellations, muttered to each other, and Rabbit, though transfixed by his love of the Sky Cabbage, realized she was beginning to hear snatches of star-talk. *Look at that doofus rabbit — light struck by an inconsiderate Dolly Parton of a cabbage.* The talk was not going well to Rabbit's ears, but she unfurled them hoping to hear enough to reply. *Doesn't she know the sky is ours? We are out in the void, taking the cold and wind. Night after night, and no gratitude, thank you, from a rabbit-person who should be singing our praises and celebrating our fires, instead of gooning at a fat cabbage with no light of its own. And furthermore,* the stars seemed to get redder, *that stupid vegetable allows something to nibble it away to nothing each and every month.* The stars then turned all their points toward Rabbit, who lowered her ears and covered them with her paws. She had always liked stars, liked lying on her back, counting and imagining, but never did she imagine she was displeasing them. Rabbit thought of all the cabbages at the surrounding farms, plenty of cabbages. She did not need the inconstant cabbage in the sky. But she did need the stars — the night would be lonely without them. And she turned her back on the cabbage, waggled her ears at the stars, signaling that she *did* love them, always looked for them in the darkened sky. She was sorry she had been thoughtless, forgotten their importance. This pleased the stars and they broke apart from their groupings, retook their places in the sky. They stoked their fires and brightened until the sky was filled with their lanterns. Rabbit sank to her knees and turned onto her back. She lay in the tall nibbling-grass and gazed overhead, cocked her ears to the sounds of stars singing their evening lullabies, until contented, Rabbit went to sleep.

TENTATIVE PASSAGE

Across the highway of your brows
a tiny spider makes its way
frail legs and brown hair intermingle
as it advances its horizontal route
and I
pretending to listen to you
am caught in the web of its wake
as it stitches together your brows
creating its own intricate spanwork.

SNAKES

Snakes it is, and it's all their fault,
sinuous as hell, when I can't sleep
and fear the slither of the highway,
so snake, smooth as a figure 8,
coils around my darkness
with its flicked tongue tasting air
and its road undulate
over tickling grass,
silky around rocks, glissading
by even the broken whiskey bottle
on its path to a sun ledge.

We've made it hard on snake who
came to enjoy that matchless garden
and got all coiled up in Eve's mess,
while other cultures
credit snake for reincarnation,
renewal, retread the tires, shuffle off
that snakeskin, deadskin, burnt skin
and come out pink and new —
live over again.

I wonder how it feels to be snake
toasting on some slick of slate in mid-afternoon,
sinking sun cool on your ribs,
cool along your tail.
How much sun does it take
to get snake through the night?

What happens in a fire
as the deer runs and the raccoon
flees on little burned hands
and the fox spins ahead of the flame;
snake will hole in, insulated
from the storm above;
snake curls in on himself
and waits it out
as he always has.

SLOTH

High in the branches of a cecropia,
the three-toed sloth clumps her silvery back,
looking like a yeti in the canopy.
She reaches out a languid, cold-molasses arm
to draw in one slender branch of breakfast.
It's like watching a nature film
in inexorable slow-motion.
This sloth may never come down
from her tree-hammock, so wary
of predators, so careful
that she only defecates during rain.
Slowly now, she turns her face toward us
gape-mouthed below in the hot fetid morning air;
reaches out her arm again, so deliberately glacial,
to pull off one small green leaf.
And we laugh to imagine her mating dance,
like Tai Chi in some misty dawn.

SAVING SPIDERS

I am doing it again,
waiting for the fairy-legged spider
to walk into my glass
so I can set her outside
among leaves,

as if I could thus
save the owls, osprey, the whales,
as if I could cup Earth
and set her safely
among the grasses.

Each morning
brings news of our declining...

The spider finding herself
on alien loam
must reconstruct
a territory, a shelter, a safety.

There are things I should be doing
but the sheer enormity
nails my feet.
I am ashamed of this carpentry.

A Saga of Sow Bugs

Sow bugs like our hot tub,
seek a moist haven under the lip of the cover.
They live there, birth there,
one large and many tiny generations.

By day they huddle,
at night they scramble out
and eat the potted pansies on the bench.

I don't want to share those yellow faces
with sow bugs. Their appreciation
is entirely gastronomic.

Each morning I step into the hot tub
and sink down. I lift the plastic combing.
Sow bugs.
Sudden exposure confuses them,
their minds go faster than their legs,
six swimming lifeguard-legs to move them
to safety.

I blow a gust of human wind and most of them
sail beyond the deck. Occasionally one falls
backward into hot water, sinks quickly.
I catch and lift it out
unfazed, legs still churning. I fling them
over the side into a one-story freefall.

I do not need their deaths,
only relocation.
What are they thinking as they fall?
Is it like a pilot:
grandeur with a bit of the usual?

Skunk in the Way

Setting off by car
I round the second bend on Spencer
and see a skunk, dead,
not yet mangled,
a black fur-piece with its bold white V
and a little wetness of blood.

Had I come sooner, I might have seen him
ambling his snuffle along the shoulder,
or worse, seen the panic
of his lack of knowledge about roads,
how he found himself trapped
against the steep side.

It's mating season for skunks — his honest
quest took him down off the hills
and into harm's way.

I hope he found her, rooting for small grubs,
scratching with her long nails to loosen dinner
from the hard dirt. I hope she found him
acceptable and gave up the night
to his insistence,

so when he reached that ribbon of asphalt
he was satisfied;
so that when he died on the second curve
he had passed on that genetic arrow,
lustrous black thick fur,
small round ears close to the head
and the panache of his tail.

"THERE IS A SNAKE WHICH HAS APPEARED HERE. COME SEE THE GOD!"
Hapur, India

Cobra winds its dry black slither up the fig tree
and settles itself in the lower branches,
which is not a good choice.

Hindus to the left hear the good news
and come to throw gold and flowers
on the tree roots. Bowls of milk
are set out for Lord Shiva.

Muslims to the right, who own the land
and therefore the tree,
and for that moment, the snake,
are offended. *This is our land.*
No temples will be built here.

Money, flowers, and gold bracelets
circle the tree;
chanting and shouts circle the branches
where the snake tries to appear
very small.

There are blows, and police come,
clanking their steel and clacking batons,
and the melee begins
to look like Sambo's tigers
running themselves into ghee.

The cobra has had enough and tries
to slither from the din, but Hindus,
not to be robbed of their fervor,
catch and toss it repeatedly
back into the tree.

Someone tries to kill the snake,
though it can not be killed, being holy.
But it is a near thing.

Rioting, noise, smoky flashes of color,
stripes of gunshot,
and the dead begin to gather:
Hindus at the tree, Muslims in the village,

and through it all the chanting
of the faithful.

But there will be no temple,
for as rioters blow about
like leaves in autumn, the cobra,
slithering silently downward.
seizes its moment to vanish.

A SQUABBLE OF SEAGULLS

MINE MINE BACK OFF
squawk seagulls as they dive
on sand and picnic blankets.
Beyond them, the sea sequins
under the sun and an occasional
sea otter pops up to inspect.

Gulls grab and insult. Each
wants every piece. The speckled
young hold back impatient,
awaiting maturity or opportunity.

The sand dithers. Gulls snatch
what they can, then grab from each other,
take their prize a little distant, while
still eying more booty.

And I remember rumbling
into New York City to engage
in the chaos of Filene's basement.

Turtle Night

Under a full moon, twenty four matrons rise from a sea
white with combers and start their slow, predestined haul
up the slope to dry sand, above the high tide mark.
Not as a squadron. But silently. Separately.

One minute she is not there, and then, in a receding wave,
a dark mass forms. Each wave leaves more of it
until a mountain of blackness, denser than steel,
moves slowly up the midnight beach.

From canyons of the sea where life is deep and unrecorded,
she is compelled back to this place of her birth
for one struggled maternal moment in the sand.
We urge her on, silently will her energy

to flipper that huge tonnage to a safe nesting spot.
We are caught in cathedral silence.
Leaving the weightless sea to pulse the cycle once again;
dragged against gravity's pull; she slips into a birthing trance.

She lays them, beneath the Southern Cross, dropping them
down the funnel into their sand chamber. Then, a barrage
of smaller eggs to blanket the clutch, to keep sand
from drifting in, to keep the nursery clear to breathe.

Gently, then firmly, she packs the nest, and swiveling a circle,
flings deceiving sand in all directions. She is magnificent.
It's two a.m. and we've been with her.
She heads back toward the sea, relentless. Down the track

she struggled so hard to climb. She smells it now:
the salt, the wetness. A forward wave curls round
her front flippers and recedes. She sighs,
a little puff of breath. She is almost there.

The next wave and the next.
She is home.
The moon paths across her shell
and she is water-borne.

TROUT SLEEPING

In the slow sun of a pool
caught behind granite, trout
slow their thoughts into long moments of sleep.
They hang in water like sleek torpedoes, light
flickering off their scales catches
the merest tempo of fins, as the pool,
calm at the top, sinks to meet
the insistent currents of the bottom.

Trout sleep
in meditation with their drift.
Their lidless eyes do not move.
Their thick meaty bodies
don't bump, nor do they
nudge the shore or snag
on roots hanging.

For this moment, they ignore larvae,
are too inward for the moth that
catches the surface and falters.
They're like the protective balloons
above the roof tops of battered England,
hung in currents of air, dancing slightly
against their long ropes, holding in place
despite what would pull them free.

WELL MET

A leatherback leaves the sand
without regret; carves her way toward
the enclasping safety of ocean depths.
At last she reaches wet sand,
where wave ends splash against her shell,
moon-brushed and stark under the Southern Cross.
We were, for a moment's black embrace,
compeers, in a place where ramblers
do not stay the course.
She had appointed rounds, and I
was her unbidden handmaiden for this night.

GOLDEN TOADS

We looked for them everywhere,
under leaves, near the springs and marshes,
the famous golden toads of Costa Rica
were gone.

We had seen in early morning the fauve
poison arrow frogs, bright spotted red,
yellow and black.

We saw fingernail frogs
living in the throats of giant leaves
a private swimming hole, dinner
tumbling down slippery.

Zoologists and bufologists
came every year, to Monte Verde,
hoping, searching, for golden toads
unseen now for five years.

All over the globe, frogs and toads
were being sucked into the void,
as if a decree had gone out, as if
a tuck had been made in this altitude.

The pools were there, deep
and coolly green in the humid forest,
the decaying edges, bugs flitting
and falling, getting caught in the water,

fat and juicy, but no toads sprang,
no spiral tongues unfurled. Gone,
with their bulgy eyes,
cocked and springy legs,
their golden skin.

Turtle Trails

And what of the turtle
who finds her trail blocked
by the new asphalt road,
hot as just poured pitch,
and she with places to go...

and what's left of the turtle
who dares the hot tar
but can't beat tires, that singing
skid year-rings off her plastron,
crack her carapace into splinters
to bleach in the sun, and egg shells
like bits of plastic, shard-sharp
in dry air...

and what of tomorrow, of next year,
when turtles no longer come this way,
their span reduced to the width of a road;
generations of turtles
smacked to the side of a road that replaced
dirt trails, that dried up wetlands,
pulled taut the hills into flatland,
ripped reed and sedge from the runnels
of waterways, that took the land
from the turtle as surely as from the Indian,
taking her eggs, and her poems.

THE AIR DANCE OF THE TURKEY VULTURE

Black leather wings
    spread to dry in the early sun,
        they perch on fences like great bat-birds.

The naked rubber head
    red, wrinkled,
        eyes piercing as Picasso's.

Tearing beak, their ripping claws
    Some disgusting temperature controls
        you don't want to think about.

But when they fly
    when they launch themselves
        like a single feather

into thermals curved as the hills below
    when they glide
        controlling the wind

by the least shift of their weight
    when they soar and begin
        the open spiral that fuels their search

then they are air creatures
    beautiful black sweeps across the sky
        efficient spectral superb

VALLON-PONT-D'ARC

They've found a network of caves full of the bones
of bears and on the walls race panthers,
shoulders curved around bulges of stilled clay.

Unimpeded by outcrops, deer leap over crevices.
Bison pick their way through the spirit world

with slender legs, and the hands that made them
are pressed brown alongside, and white below
and among are hands blown in red outline,

and in this cave, the one just found, the one
we'll never see because of our soggy exhale,

the mammoths are free to lumber, horses gallop
and in the meager light
wooly-haired rhinoceros, here, in southern Europe,

their scimitar horns stabbing forward above fat lips,
their eyes squinted, and near them,

a red slouching hyena some artist slipped among the rumps
and manes he was taught to draw as we were taught
to form our letters plump and even

along two solid blue lines and one dotted — and overhead
where the handmaiden of darkness is most at home,

flies an owl — a sage to control the jokester? —
while on the ceiling, horses float on their cream-colored
hooves like waves on an ocean of stone.

Someone stumbled into this hole, down the unexpected
like Alice tumbling after rabbits with watches. They slipped

like spilled ink into the veins of earth and found the lost herds,
shined a thin pencil of light into the widened eyes of horses,
their snorting nostrils and sooty manes, their speckled flanks.

MOUTH OF THE WHALE

They meet in open ocean:
the fishermen insistent about their net,
the cetalogists insistent upon the whale,
the humpback insistent on living.

The whale is entangled,
the net wrapped on her pectoral flipper,
snarled in her baleen.
Its weight drags her down.

She struggles up, twisting: caught fast.
The net is huge and costly,
what is one whale to such
investment, their livelihood?
On another day, the whale
would forfeit to their net but today
the fishermen pull their boat back, waiting.

One wild eye watches
the approach of the scientists' boat.
They probe at the net, crusted, cold,
work it slowly free of the flipper.
The whale quiets: some.

They approach her mouth.
She waits.
Her baleen can't be reached from the boat.
One man is frightened but willing.
The whale parts her jaws, holds them
above the water. The man
crawls onto the whale's tongue.

One man
One whale

Above are the long tangles,
beyond is the sloped cave
of the throat, below a dark trench
in the sea. Jonah

How slowly he works, careful.
The net begins to fall loose.
He finishes what he can reach
then feels the hydraulics of the tongue
lifting him. He continues.

The net's weight
is pulling the whale down. She urges
with her tongue, pushes the man out
and sinks below the swells.

Time hangs in the air,
the fishermen groan at the loss of their net,
the scientists are quiet.

She's coming up, Thrashes to the surface
and opens her mouth. The man
climbs back in, balances again
on the thick muscle of the tongue,
continues his work and finally

the net falls away,
fishermen scrambling to secure it.
The whale waits while the Zodiak
draws near and the man
backs through yards of hanging keratin
and leaves the mouth of the whale.

A GAM OF WHALES

Whales gambol through wave breaks
like semi-trailers pulling into
a roadside diner.
As long ago, two boats of whalers
hove to across an open sea,
spars on the horizon joining
for a gam, as crews lofted
back and forth in a gamming chair
over the inky sea; and out came
the rum, the news, and
tall tales of Nantucket sleigh rides.
Do whales exchange the news
while bubbling together for fish?
We know that they sing.

Tribal Totem

Older sister of the coyote, and not above
being the trickster to some, Lobo, the wolf
enters California from the North, on her own,
bringing healing powers of the Makah.

Tribal totem girl, with the bear and the raven
holding the tundra, raising the river current
so salmon can ride it home.

Soft padding through short grasses on your tour
of duty and hunger — looking for family.
It was you, as Lupa, who restored Romulus
and his brother. Lupa, who raised those two
and created the City upon the Seven Hills.

Step back Aeneus — Johnny come lately — Lupa
gets the credit. Medicine maker, cloaked
in wraps of gray, she stalks the wary rabbit,
jumps the silly bird that nests on ground, rolls
as a gray streak through hills of spruce
and blinding snow.

Sniffs into burrows, under the flakes of needles,
lifting her voice into the rough-ready wind,
up to the stars in a howl seeking connection.
She and her sisters, alpha pack-mates, raising
the generations, sending them out
across the spring land to start anew.

WOLF

The ratchet of her voice
slides over the pack
in easy strokes of the wind.

She howls for her mate
lost to the hunter.

She calls for her pups
and her sisters to come closer

into the lee of an outcrop
where the ice slivers
that fill the air to denseness
fall silent beneath the overhang.

She is the moon's sister
and the song of the outback.

She was forbidden the canyons
of the Yellowstone, and hunted from the tundra

and stories told of her are the lies
on which the hunters feast.

And I love her,
the silver tips of her coarse hair,

the right-angled brow
sheltering eyes yellow as tourmaline

and the broad reach of snout
leaning into tales carried on the wind.

And we hunt her — drive her
from her land, take over the rocks,
plow the tree stands into meadow,
civilize the ground, and prefer
not to know how much she is like us.

THE YELLOW JACKET

I go to the rain barrel
to pull a bucket, and
see a spinning yellow jacket
feebled from his long
futile swim.
A big one too.
He would as soon sting me
as eat, but now his mind
is entirely on eternal things.

I offer him a boxwood twig,
one leaf for purchase,
but he can't hold;
his legs scissor him
in weak circles, and carefully,
I offer him both twig
and hand and bring him out.
Such a little thing to me
and everything to him.

CONVOCATION

So, Whale —
we, magnanimous man,
resolve to save you,
who does not need saving
only to be left alone
to roam oceans we
only begin to understand,
even as we alter them for ourselves.

Ho, Bear.
We scoop your land
and make it exclusive.
We can't even agree
to save you —
though all you ask
is range and acceptance.
You are unlikely
to get it from us.

And Tree
we can't see for the forest;
we are hungry for lumber.
You, a whole universe
in one sky-reaching shaft
your habitations below the earth
and in your branching limbs
whole ecologies —
when you fall
and you will
with our help, our axe,
we'll lose your complete world
along with our breath.

ONCE HERE

**From an article recently written by a man of 87
who grew up in our town, our area,
and he wrote with such poignancy**

about all the bears (now gone)
in the forests (now gone),
how we used to look up at sunset
and see them silhouetted on the ridge lines
against the dusky sky.

How great troupes of elk (now gone)
used to come down to the creeks
(now gone or buried or channeled) to drink.

How the rivers (now trickles)
used to be filled with salmon (now few)
struggling their way upstream
to the source of their cycles.

How much we have lost,
and soon
will no longer even know
we have lost it.

MOONSONGS

What uncovers the long stretch of wind
that pulses from the western sea
and parts the night into hours and seconds?
Delivered on its long arms
are the moonsongs of Indians
calling ghosts of our ancestors
to gather in a circle of sage and remembrance.
From below, deep in Earth's navel,
a bell sings its high sweet communion.
Break from your usual byways
and consider the stories of eagle and wolf,
how they surround you with courage,
lift you above the long slopes of the mountains.
Given this, the wind becomes creator and guide.
Sing it your songs, tell it your tales,
add them to the universal tongue.

NOAH THROWS IN THE HAMMER

Sometime in the future, Noah will shut down
his shop, pull wood plugs from the boards,
let caulking fall as it will, take apart
stalls and fodder racks.

Shem and Ham will loosen planks
where they have weathered together,
tapping them with a handy branch.
"Good wood there, boys."
Stack them carelessly on shore
not caring if neighbors make off with them.

Sometime in the future we will have forgotten
that unicorns did not come quick-stepping
along the path, but were distracted by spring
and missed the boat, because by then

there won't be elephants or pandas who lumber
after bamboo, or tigers to blend their stripes
into the dapples of forests no longer there.

Wolves won't raise their songs to
the hidden stars; no earred seals,
geese two by two, whales and dolphins
with their hyper-brains.

Only we will be left
to worry about rising water or how difficult
it is becoming to draw a full breath or how
the only animals our daughters have ever seen
are domesticated, tame as dogs.

Somewhere in the future we'll give up
cows because with their four legs
and grass-devouring mouths they take up
too much room where we stand

thigh to thigh on barren ground
awaiting the last trumpet, though who
has any breath left to blow it,
with all their lungs sucking in oxygen,
no longer able to give out carbon dioxide
because what, after all, is left to use it.

PUBLICATION ACKNOWLEDGEMENTS
WITH THANKS

**A Cat Who Falls from a Tree Branch Will always Pretend
He Meant to** *Cat Who Says No to Schroedinger; Cat with No
Need of a Fiddle*

Acorn *Copper Flash*

Black Hills Audubon Society *The Air Dance of the Turkey Vulture;
At the Window*

Blessed Pests *A Saga of Sow Bugs*

California Quarterly *A Moment in the Marsh; Trout Sleeping*

Coracle *Snakes*

Cyclamens and Swords *Tentative Passage*

Dog Blessings *On Limantour Beach; Off the Trail*

Dualities: Nine Poets, Nine Images *Coyote Skull*

Echo; Exit 13; Wild Earth *Turtle Night*

Fish Dance *Hawk Soaring*

Grrrrr, A Collection of Poems about Bears *The Dancing Bear*

Green Fuse *Skunk in the Way; Turtle Trails; In the
Mouth of the Whale*

Icarus *Bolinas Lagoon*

In Posse Review *The Owl is a Poem*

**International Journal of Turtle and Tortoise, Chelonian
Conservation and Biology** *Turtle Trails*

Liberty Hill; Poetry Magazine.com *Like a Little Lighthouse*

Marin Poetry Center Anthology *Six Horses; Considering
Endless Night*

New Works Review *A School of Koi, Pausing*

Of Frogs and Toads *Longest Leap Outside Calaveras;
Frogs and Geraniums*

Onion River Review *Catching Fish*

Orange C *Pieces of Conscience*

Pegasus Review; Emily Dickinson Award Anthology,
    Best Poems of 1996   *The Yellow Jacket* (The Wasp)
Pennine Platford *At the Window*
Poems for a Livable Planet   *Well–Met*
Power of Poetry; Ribet; Ruah IV   *St. Francis Day*
Psychological Perspective   *Night Bear*
Pudding House Gang   *Turnabout Being Fair Play*
Red Owl Magazine   *Wolf*
RUNES, A Review of Poetry   *Connection*
Rockford Review   *Rivertrail*
Snowy Egret   *If I*
South Coast Review; Pudding House   *"There is a Snake*
    Which Has Appeared Here. Come See the God!"
Spillway   *A Storm of Feathers or Suddenly, Feathers , A Cloud of Bats;*
    Flight Feather; A Cloud of Grasshoppers, A Labor of Moles
Standing Wave   *Trout Sleeping*
Texas Poetry Calendar   *Cows*
Tiger's Eye   *Oracle Bones*
Women Artist Datebook   *One Bird Falling*
Word Outta Buffalo; New Verse News   *Raptors*
Wordplay   *Sloth*
Xenophilia; Grrrrr, A Collection of Poems about Bears
    Winter Bears

POETRY BOOKS BY CB FOLLETT

BOOKS

The Latitudes of Their Going (1993)
Gathering the Mountains (1995)
Visible Bones (1998)
At the Turning of the Light (National Poetry Book
    Award Winner) (2001)
Hold and Release (2007)
And Freddie Was My Darling (2008)
One Bird Falling (2011)
Of Gravity and Tides (2013)
Duet: A Conversation of Words and Images (2014)
    (with Ginna Fleming, photographer)
Quatrefoil (2016)

CHAPBOOKS

CB Follett's Greatest Hits (2001)
Runaway Girl (2008)
Houses (2011)
Boxing the Compass
    Compass Points (2011)
    Compass Rose (2013)
    True North (2014)
    Wind Rose (2014)

CHAPBOOKS (limited edition, handsewn)

Bull Kelp (1996)

Nightmare Fish (2002)

Vallon Pont d'Arc (2003)

Arms (2003)

Hermit Crab (2003)

Duxbury Reef (2003)

Wheels (2003)

The Loving of Trees (2007)

A Cat Who Falls from a Tree Branch Will Always
     Claim He Meant To (2008)

Poems to Red Rocks (2009)

ABOUT THE AUTHOR & THE ARTIST

CB FOLLETT

is the author of 10 books of poems, including **Quatrefoil** (2016), and several chapbooks, most recently the **Boxing The Compass** series (2014-15). **At The Turning of The Light** won the National Poetry Book Award. She is the Editor/Publisher of Arctos Press, was publisher and co-editor (with Susan Terris) of **Runes**, a Review of Poetry (2001-2007). Follett has nine nominations for Pushcart Prizes for individual poems, as well as ten nominations as an individual poet; a Marin Arts Council Grant for Poetry; awards and honors; and has been widely published both nationally and internationally. Follett was Poet Laureate of Marin County, CA (2010-2013).

JOYCE KOSKENMAKI

has exhibited her art both nationally and internationally and won many grants and awards. Her work is included in numerous public and private collections.